HARD ROCK
JAM ALONG

by Marc "Coop" Cooper

Unlock your improvisational ability.
Play along to seven hard rock tracks recorded in realtime by real musicians.
Loaded with chord diagrams, full progressions, scale and arpeggio choices,
and great ideas for soloing over each tune.

SO-BZC-306

AMSCO PUBLICATIONS
New York/London/Sydney

Cat Character: **Marc "Coop" Cooper**
Layout & Production: **Tammy Blake**
Photography: **Martin Love**
Text Editing: **Tammy Blake**

Musicians on CD:
Guitars, Guitar EFX, Harmonized guitars, bass: **Marc "Coop" Cooper**
Drums: **Attila Turi, Jeff Salem**

Copyright © 1991, 1996 by Music Education Workshop Inc.™
This Book Published 1996 by Amsco Publications,
A Division of Music Sales Corporation, New York, NY.

All Rights Reserved. No part of this book may be reproduced in any form
or by any electronic or mechanical means, including information storage
and retrieval systems, without permission in writing from the publisher.

Order Number: AM 931359
US International Standard Book Number: 0.8256.1498.8
UK International Standard Book Number: 0.7119.5136.5

Exclusive Distributors:
Music Sales Corporation
257 Park Avenue South, New York, NY 10010 USA
Music Sales Limited
8/9 Frith Street, London W1V 5TZ England
Music Sales Pty. Limited
120 Rothschild Street, Rosebery, Sydney NSW 2018, Australia

Printed in the United States of America by
Vicks Lithograph and Printing Corporation

TABLE OF CONTENTS and ORDER OF CD

The last track on the CD is Coop jamming out and having fun to **The Grooveyard** progression.

Preface

Hard rock and heavy metal music has always had a strong, loyal following. I started out learning the tunes of Deep Purple, Led Zeppelin, Hendrix, Focus, anything that I could crank it out to. Jimmy Page, Ritchie Blackmore, Jan Akkerman, Hendrix (of course!), Jeff Beck, Pat Travers, Pat Thrall, Brian May, Alex Lifeson, Kim Mitchell, and Frank Marino were some of my early influences. Later on Eddie Van Halen, Gary Moore, Joe Satriani, Steve Vai, Yngwie Malmsteen, Nuno Bettencourt, Jennifer Batten, John Sykes, Paul Gilbert, and many other hot shredders of the 80s brought technical and advanced improvisational skills to the genre. Thrash, speed metal, grunge, or whatever you want to call it has brought some interesting and diverse players to the arena as well. In the end it's all about cranking it out, turning up to 11, wailing out heavy riffs (drivin' your parents crazy!), and trying to play with some reckless abandon and emotion.

Many of my students only wanted to play heavy metal songs. They had no interest in learning how scales, licks, chords, and arpeggios could be incorporated into this style to help improve and expand their musical vision and thus allow them to grow. Students would come up to me and play a Van Halen tapping riff but not know how to incorporate it into their playing: They'd try playing as fast as they could and end up not making much sense because they didn't know how to play through changes and progressions. They didn't understand how it all fits and works together. This Jam Along is designed to get you to play through different chord changes, different tempos, new progressions (possibly ones that you haven't played through before) and learn new scales, patterns and different arpeggios.

I think it's important to develop good practice habits. I suggest that practicing with a metronome and warming up before you jam will help you with the technical side. Working on alternate picking (up/down;down/up) is helpful. Knowing what it is you want to get out of your practice session will help you to focus on the areas you need to work on. Try practicing the scales and arpeggios in triplets, sequences, or sextuplets. Try string skipping the scales or sweeping the arpeggios to create your own new licks. Try learning these patterns up and down the fretboard linearly instead of just across the neck. Try learning your arpeggios up and down the fretboard on one or two strings.

Above all, listen to the changes so you can hear when the progression moves, and make sure you change your scales, arpeggios, or chords to fit the progressions. Learn to recognize different chords and when the chords are changing. Learn to hear what a harmonic minor scale or some of the more exotic scales (Phrygian, Dorian, Mixolydian) sound like. Learn to distinguish between a major blues scale and minor blues scale. Listening to as many styles of music as you can will help you to avoid playing the same old clichés and licks.

Oh yeah, this CD is designed to work best if you crank it and turn your amp all the way up to 20 ! Blast away on some righteous rude riffs, dude! Enjoy the head banging.

Coop

Marc "Coop" Cooper

JAM - ALONG SONG NOTES

It's advantageous to read these liner notes before tackling these Jam Along progressions. This will help you to get a better picture of how I put them together. I've written these hard rock progressions in different keys to help you break stale soloing habits caused from playing in the same key all the time (many beginning guitarists tend to play only in the keys of A or E).

The primary scale choices I've suggested are pentatonic and blues scales, but I've also emphasized some modal scales. The harmonic minor scale is another scale I use frequently. If you are unfamiliar with the five finger patterns of each of these scales or the three-note-per-string patterns of the modes (major, harmonic minor, or melodic minor) you will find my book, *Scale Vocabulary*, helpful.

Hard rock doesn't have to be the same old boring riffs and grooves: Here are some additional notes for the progressions in this book. The chord types for these progressions are primarily power chords, (root and 5th) or they are simply triads (three note chords) over different bass notes (slash chords). If you aren't familiar with these kinds of chords you find my book *Chord Vocabulary* helpful. It will give you a solid background in understanding the nature of chords and their relationships.

All of the scale and arpeggio choices in this Jam Along are only suggestions. As you grow as a player, your own vocabulary of licks and ideas will increase and you will want to try your own choices.

Metalizer: This progression is split up into three sections (A, B, C). Section A is based on Dm with a power-chord riff using D5, E5, F5. Throughout this section (every time it comes around) you can use the D blues scale or the D Aeolian minor. This indicates that you treat this as the key of D minor which is the relative minor key to F major, or the sixth mode of the key of F, you can also use the D harmonic minor scale for this section.

Section B is based in the keys of E and G. For E you can use a modal approach using the modes E Ionian, B Mixolydian, and A Lydian. All these modes are based on the E major scale. For G you can use the modes based on the G major scale (G Ionian, D Mixolydian, C Lydian).

Section C (which happens twice in the tune) is based on a minor pentatonic riff. The D minor pentatonic and D blues scales work well over this riff.

Regarding arpeggios; note that as with scales, there are five different finger patterns for every arpeggio type based on where the five root-note patterns are. Some patterns, such as in this song, are more linear in their approach designed to cover more of the fretboard. I've included most of these finger patterns (for major, minor, minor 7, and dominant 7 arpeggios) throughout the book. I suggest transposing the different patterns into the different progressions for each song so you can become comfortable with every pattern by memory. In Section B, the B chord and the D chord are really just passing chords. I would concentrate on the first and fourth arpeggios in E and G. Since section C is geared more for scale soloing than arpeggio soloing, only the arpeggios for Sections A and B are included.

Snakebite: This progression is split up into two sections (A and B). Section A is based in the key of G (with the exception of the F5 chord). Section B is a funk groove based around the F blues scale utilizing the chords F, E♭, B♭, A♭.

With the exception of the Am7 and Bm7, all of the arpeggios are major triad (three-note) arpeggios.

Psychedelic Relic: This minor blues has a few twists in it. The progression is essentially a Im IVm V7 except that in between the Im and IVm chord a ♭IIIm chord has been inserted. The chords that are played over the riff were created with the Digitech DHP 33 Harmonizer. You could analyze the chord structures I created with the harmonizer so you could understand how I made my arpeggio choices.

That's enough to get you started; the remaining songs are discussed within the body of the book. I encourage everyone who jams along to this CD, if there are sections of this book you don't understand, go to a teacher and have them explain it to you. You can learn so much quicker when you have an experienced guide to help you through a difficult passage.

If you have any suggestions for any other kinds of Jam Along books that you would like to see, feel free to write me at the following addresses below.

In the U.S:
M.E.O.W.
Music Education Workshop
3380 Sheridan Dr STE#414
Amherst, N.Y.
USA 14226

In Canada:
M.E.O.W.
Music Education Workshop
Box 1219
Burlington, Ontario
Canada L7R 4L8

REMEMBER, BE AN INNOVATOR NOT AN IMITATOR !

Metalizer

"Metalizer" starts with a sixteen-bar progression in D minor. The type of chords used are two-note power chords, sometimes called diads. You could pick and mute the open D string and play the two note chords as shown.

Scale Choices

Section A

The scale choices for Section A are:

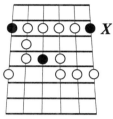

D Blues Scale

● =Root (tonic note)

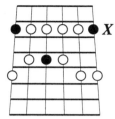

D Minor Pentatonic

● =Root (tonic note)

D Blues:	D	F	G	A♭	A	C
Interval Structure:	R	♭3	4	♭5	5	♭7

D Minor Pentatonic:	D	F	G	A	C
Interval Structure:	R	♭3	4	5	♭7

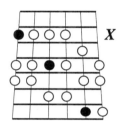

D Aeolian Minor

● =Root (tonic note)

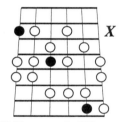

D Harmonic Minor

● =Root (tonic note)

D Aeolian Minor:	D	E	F	G	A	B♭	C
Interval Structure:	R	2	♭3	4	5	♭6	♭7

D Harmonic Minor:	D	E	F	G	A	B♭	C#
Interval Structure:	R	2	♭3	4	5	♭6	7

Arpeggio Choices

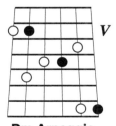

Dm Arpeggio

● =Root (tonic note)

Dm Arpeggio

● =Root (tonic note)

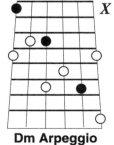

Dm Arpeggio

● =Root (tonic note)

Dm Arpeggio:	D	F	A
Interval Structure:	R	♭3	5

Scale Choices

Section B

Section B is sixteen bars also. Here the tune changes from minor to major and modulates up to E and then to G.

The E major scale can be played over the E, B, and A major chords. If you start on the notes B or A (when you are playing the E major scale), you are playing the B Mixolydian mode or the A Lydian mode. For G, D, and C, you can use the G major scale. If you start on the notes D or C, (when you are playing the G Major scale), you are playing the D Mixolydian mode or the C Lydian mode. Transpose these patterns G Ionian, D Mixolydian, and C Lydian.

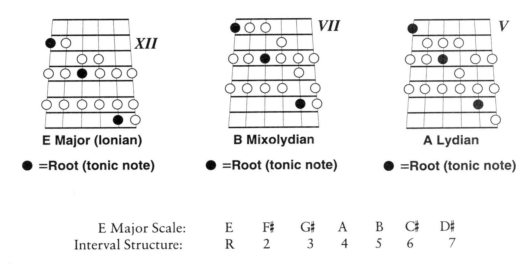

E Major Scale:	E	F♯	G♯	A	B	C♯	D♯
Interval Structure:	R	2	3	4	5	6	7

Arpeggio Choices

Remember that the chords move quickly so you won't be able to play the entire pattern. Strive for smoothness when you change arpeggios.

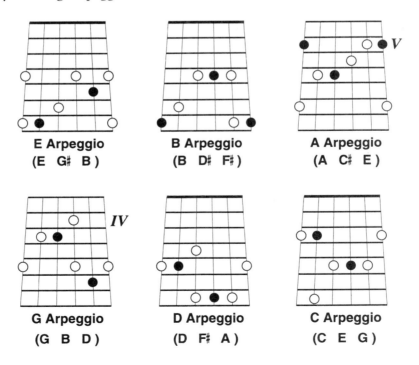

Section C consists of a riff based on D minor pentatonic. The D minor pentatonic or the D blues scale will work over these riffs.

Snakebite

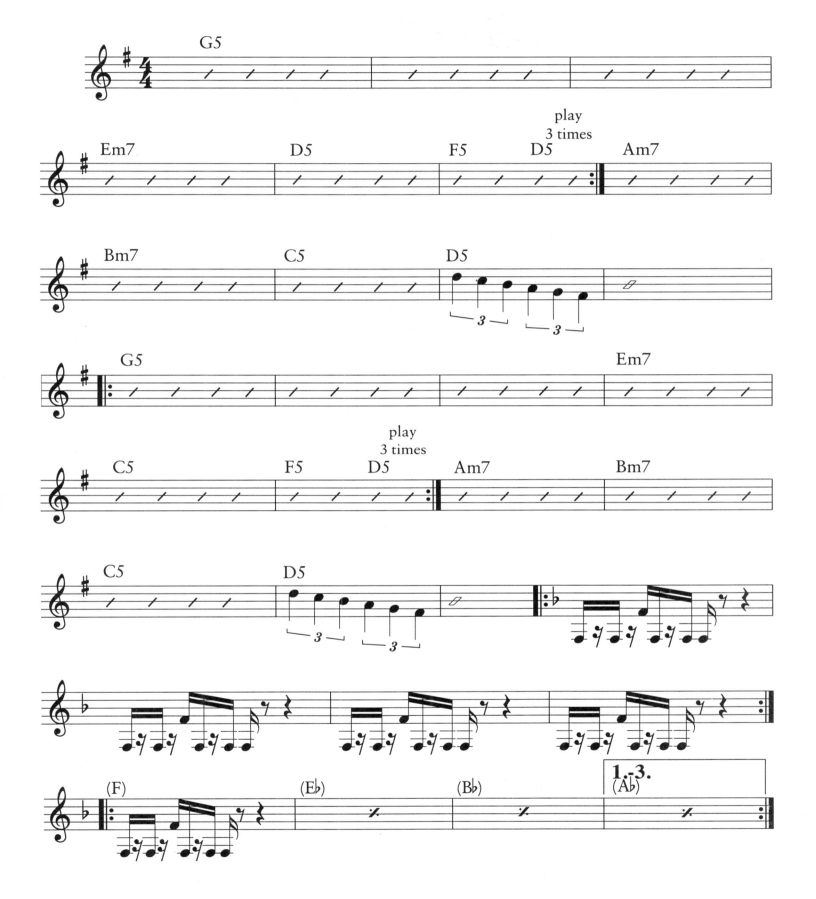

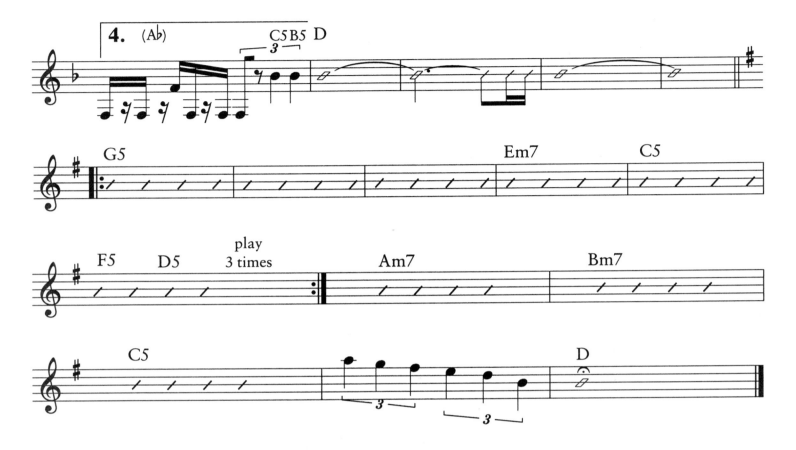

This progression can be broken down into two sections. Section A is a modal progression in the key of G: I VIm7 IV * V. The * indicates that the F5 is not in the key of G. Even though it is a power chord I've treated it like a F major chord. It is very common in songwriting to add some chords that are not in the key of the song. You can try an A blues or D blues scale against the F5 chord.

Scale Choices

This progression has a definite major tonality to it. Try the E blues scale for G5, Em7, and C5. You can also try the A blues for C5, F5, and D5.

E Blues:	E	G	A	B♭	B	D
Interval Structure						
Against G5 chord:	6	R	9	♭3/#9	3	5
Against Em7 chord:	R	♭3	4	♭5	5	♭7
Against C5 chord:	3	5	6	♭7	7	9

A Blues:	A	C	D	E♭	E	G
Interval Structure						
Against C5 chord:	6	R	9	♭3	3	5
Against F5 chord:	3	5	6	♭7	7	9
Against D5 chord:	5	♭7	R	♭9	9	4

Try the G major scale for the first three chords. Remember that as the chords change you start to play modally. What I mean is from the G5 chord to the Em7 chord to C5 your tonic notes change accordingly (G, E, C). So, modally you are playing: G Ionian, E Aeolian (minor), and C Lydian. These can be thought of as the G major scale starting on different notes of that scale.

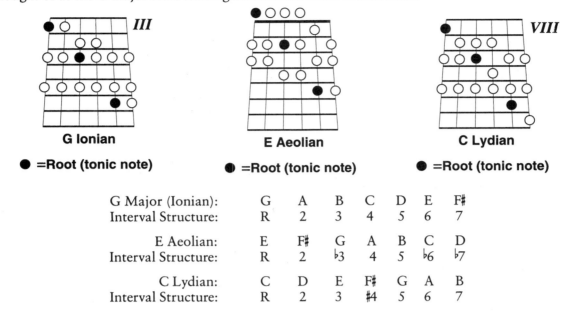

G Ionian

● =Root (tonic note)

E Aeolian

◐ =Root (tonic note)

C Lydian

● =Root (tonic note)

G Major (Ionian):	G	A	B	C	D	E	F#
Interval Structure:	R	2	3	4	5	6	7
E Aeolian:	E	F#	G	A	B	C	D
Interval Structure:	R	2	♭3	4	5	♭6	♭7
C Lydian:	C	D	E	F#	G	A	B
Interval Structure:	R	2	3	#4	5	6	7

Since the F5 and D5 chords happen quite quickly (two beats each), I suggest trying the D blues scale for both chords.

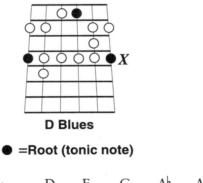

D Blues

● =Root (tonic note)

D Blues:	D	F	G	A♭	A	C
Interval Structure						
Against F5 chord:	6	R	9	♭3/#9	3	5
Against D5 chord:	R	♭3/#9	4	♭5	5	♭7

For Am7, try A Dorian. For Bm7, try B Phrygian.

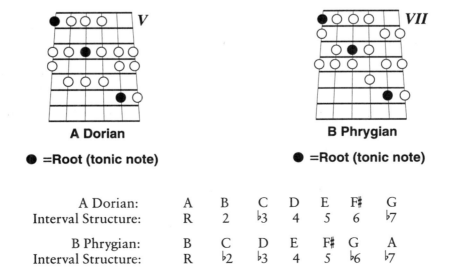

A Dorian

● =Root (tonic note)

B Phrygian

● =Root (tonic note)

A Dorian:	A	B	C	D	E	F#	G
Interval Structure:	R	2	♭3	4	5	6	♭7
B Phrygian:	B	C	D	E	F#	G	A
Interval Structure:	R	♭2	♭3	4	5	♭6	♭7

Try the A minor pentatonic scale for Am7 and C5, and the B minor pentatonic scale for Bm7 and D5.

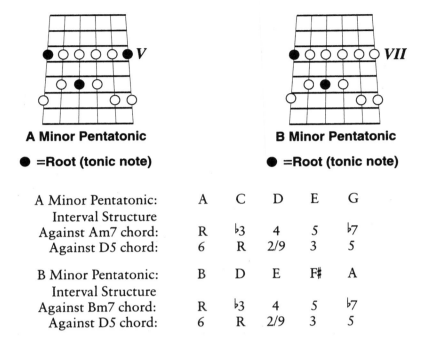

A Minor Pentatonic

● =Root (tonic note)

B Minor Pentatonic

● =Root (tonic note)

A Minor Pentatonic:	A	C	D	E	G
Interval Structure					
Against Am7 chord:	R	♭3	4	5	♭7
Against D5 chord:	6	R	2/9	3	5
B Minor Pentatonic:	B	D	E	F♯	A
Interval Structure					
Against Bm7 chord:	R	♭3	4	5	♭7
Against D5 chord:	6	R	2/9	3	5

Arpeggio Choices

Section A

Try a G major arpeggio for G5 and Em7.

G Arpeggio

● =Root (tonic note)

G Arpeggio:	G	B	D
Interval Structure:	R	3	5
Interval Structure			
Against Em7:	♭3	5	♭7

x = you can add the root of the Em7 if you want to.

For C5, try the C major arpeggio.

For F5, try F major.

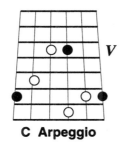

C Arpeggio

● =Root (tonic note)

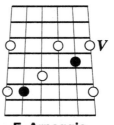

F Arpeggio

● =Root (tonic note)

C Arpeggio:	C	E	G
Interval Structure:	R	3	5

F Arpeggio:	F	A	C
Interval Structure:	R	3	5

Move the F major arpeggio down three frets to play a D major arpeggio over the D5.

Here are some arpeggios to use over the chords to the second part of the A Section.

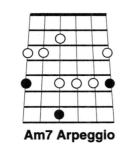

Am7 Arpeggio

● =Root (tonic note)

Bm7 Arpeggio

● =Root (tonic note)

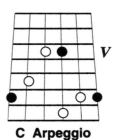

C Arpeggio

● =Root (tonic note)

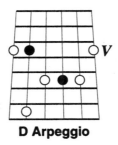

D Arpeggio

● =Root (tonic note)

Scale Choices
Section B

For the eight bars of the static F-note funk rhythm the chords haven't been established yet. You can try the F blues scale.

F Blues:	F	A♭	B♭	C♭	C	E♭
Interval Structure:	R	♭3(♯9)	4	♭5	5	♭7

When the chords are introduced, try the F blues scale throughout the entire progression. Here are some additional F blues patterns.

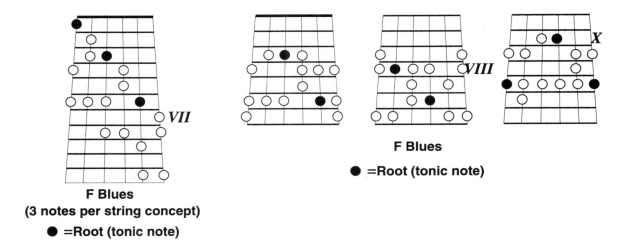

F Blues
(3 notes per string concept)
● =Root (tonic note)

F Blues
● =Root (tonic note)

For the four bars of D try the B blues scale.

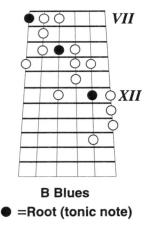

B Blues
● =Root (tonic note)

B Blues:	B	D	E	F	F♯	A
Interval Structure Against D:	6	R	9	♭3(♯9)	3	5

Arpeggio Choices

Section B

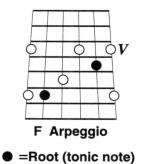

F Arpeggio

● =Root (tonic note)

F Arpeggio:	F	A	C
Interval Structure:	R	3	5

E♭ Major Arpeggio

● =Root (tonic note)

E♭ Arpeggio:	E♭	G	B♭
Interval Structure:	R	3	5

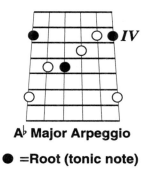

A♭ Major Arpeggio

● =Root (tonic note)

A♭ Arpeggio:	A♭	C	E♭
Interval Structure:	R	3	5

B♭ Major Arpeggio

● =Root (tonic note)

B♭ Arpeggio:	B♭	G	F
Interval Structure:	R	3	5

Psychedelic Relic

This is a twenty four- bar minor progression in Gminor (a twisted blues?!), and in this progression
we'll look at the blues scale. (You can never get away from the blues!)
It starts with a riff played once through before other chords are superimposed over top.
This riff continues, with variations, throughout the tune.

Scale Choices

First the blues scale. For the Gm(Im), Cm(IVm), and D7(V7) chords, try the G blues scale.

For the B♭m chord, try the B♭ blues scale.

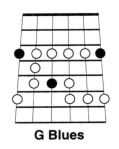

G Blues

● =Root (tonic note)

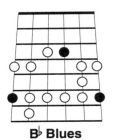

B♭ Blues

● =Root (tonic note)

G Blues :	G	B♭	C	D♭	D	F
Interval Structure :	R	♭3	4	♭5	5	♭7

B♭ Blues :	B♭	D♭	E♭	F♭	F	A♭
Interval Structure :	R	♭3	4	♭5	5	♭7

For the IVm(Cm) chord, you could also try the C blues scale.

For the V7(D7) chord, you could also try the D blues scale.

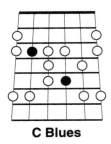

C Blues

● =Root (tonic note)

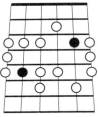

D Blues

● =Root (tonic note)

C Blues :	C	E♭	F	G♭	G	B♭
Interval Structure :	R	♭3/♯9	4	♭5	5	♭7

D Blues :	D	F	G	A♭	A	C
Interval Structure :	R	♭3/♯9	4	♭5	5	♭7

You could also try G minor pentatonic (Im), B♭ minor pentatonic; C minor pentatonic (IVm), and D minor pentatonic (V7) over these chords. The interval structure for each minor pentatonic scale is the same as the corresponding blues scale without the flatted fifth.

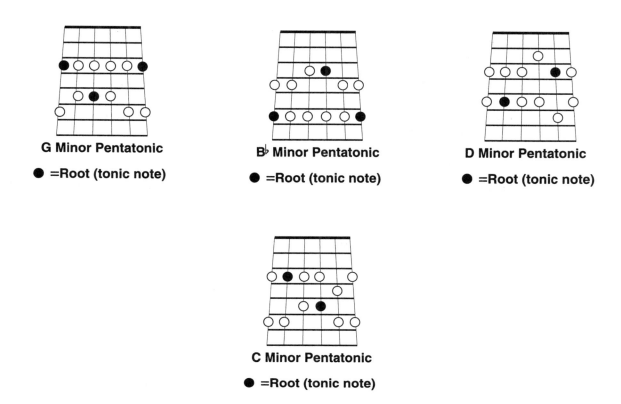

Arpeggio Choices

If you follow along with the chords written on top of the chart you could also try learning these chord arpeggios and approach it chord by chord.

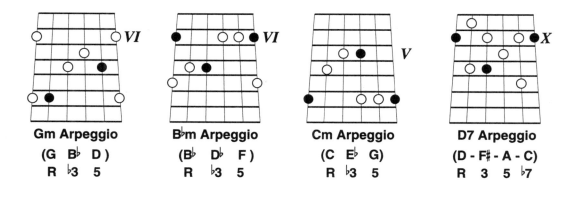

Salamander Sauce

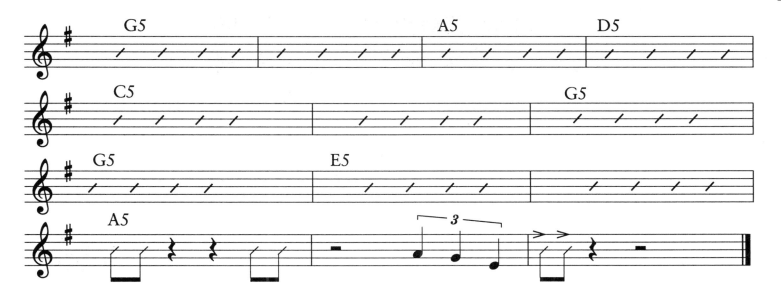

Solo Section

There are twelve bars starting this solo section: four bars of hi hat, four bars of hi hat and bass; four bars of hi hat, bass, and guitar. Even though there aren't any chords, the riff implies a D7 chord and you can try the D blues scale or the D Mixolydian scale.

Scale Choices
Solo Section

The solo section is split up into A,B,C, with C being a repeat of the A section. Since these are power chords (root and 5th—no 3rds to indicate whether they are major or minor, the tonality is open to interpretation.

One possibility is to consider that the progression is in G.

C5	G5	C5	A5	D5	C5	G5	E5	A5
IV	I	IV	II	V	IV	I	VIm	IIm

For C5(IV), G5(I), A5(II), and D5(V), try these major pentatonic scales.

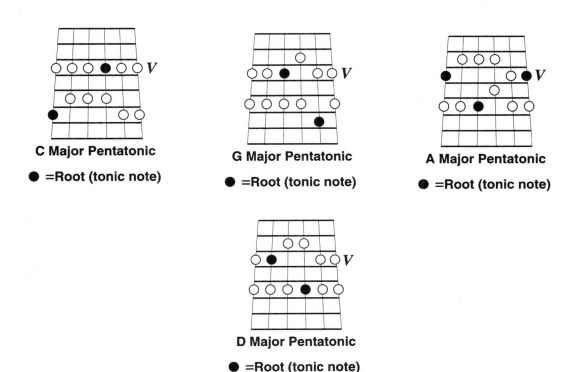

C Major Pentatonic

● =Root (tonic note)

G Major Pentatonic

● =Root (tonic note)

A Major Pentatonic

● =Root (tonic note)

D Major Pentatonic

● =Root (tonic note)

For E5(VIm), A5(IIm), and try these minor pentatonic scales.

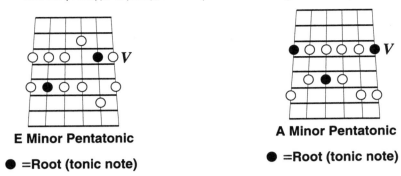

E Minor Pentatonic

● =Root (tonic note)

A Minor Pentatonic

● =Root (tonic note)

Or you can try them with a major blues scale:

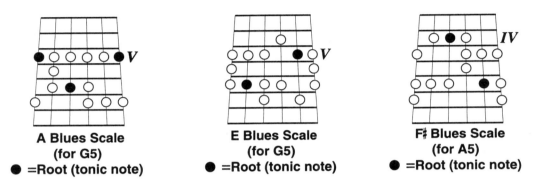

**A Blues Scale
(for G5)**
● =Root (tonic note)

**E Blues Scale
(for G5)**
● =Root (tonic note)

**F♯ Blues Scale
(for A5)**
● =Root (tonic note)

Creates a C major blues sound.   Creates a G major blues sound.   Creates an A♯ major blues sound.

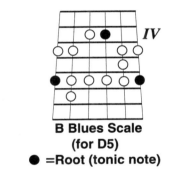

**B Blues Scale
(for D5)**
● =Root (tonic note)

Creates a D major blues sound.

and for the last two chords E5 (VIm) and A5 (IIm) try:

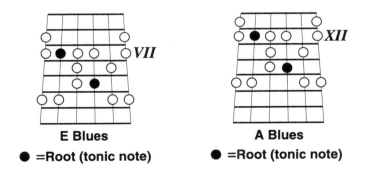

E Blues

● =Root (tonic note)

A Blues

● =Root (tonic note)

Scale Choices   Section B

E5	D5	A5	G5
VIm	V	IIm	I

Try the E minor pentatonic or E blues for E5, D major pentatonic or B blues for D5, A minor pentatonic or A blues for A5, and G major pentatonic or E blues for G5.

Arpeggio Choices for Section A

I've implied major-chord arpeggios over the power chords, and for the second G chord I've implied a G7 arpeggio.

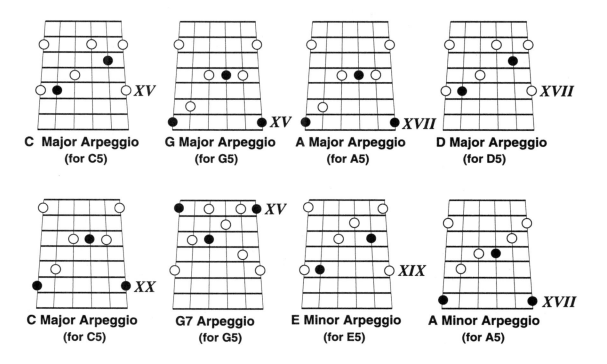

Arpeggio Choices for Section B

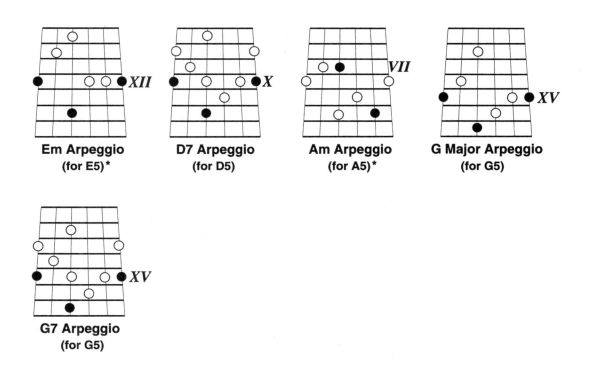

Rock Steady

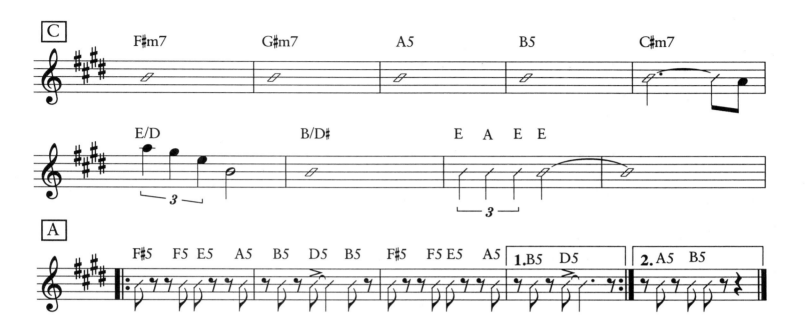

Section A of this progression is based on the A blues scale. Section B is a V IV I progression in D. Section C introduces a modal progression: II III IV V VI I7 V I .

Each section generally is eight bars in length, though sometimes section A is sixteen bars in length. After 120 bars it modulates up a whole step to the key of B. At this point, all of the scale and arpeggio choices may be moved up two frets on the fingerboard; for example, the A blues at the 5th fret will now be moved up to a B blues scale at the 7th fret.

Chords for Section B.

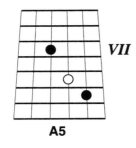

A5

● =Root (tonic note)

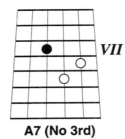

A7 (No 3rd)

● =Root (tonic note)

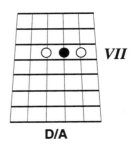

D/A

● =Root (tonic note)

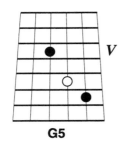

G5

● =Root (tonic note)

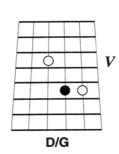

D/G

● =Root (tonic note)

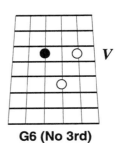

G6 (No 3rd)

● =Root (tonic note)

Chords for Section C.

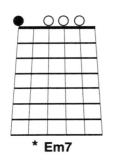

* Em7

● =Root (tonic note)

F♯m7

● =Root (tonic note)

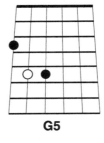

G5

● =Root (tonic note)

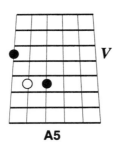

A5

● =Root (tonic note)

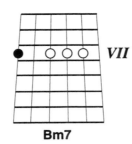

Bm7

● =Root (tonic note)

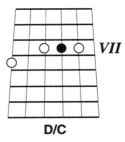

D/C

● =Root (tonic note)

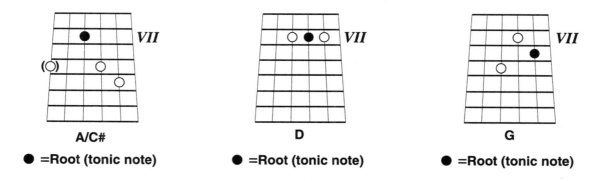

A/C#   D   G

● =Root (tonic note)   ● =Root (tonic note)   ● =Root (tonic note)

Scale Choices for Section A.

These are suggested scale choices, there are others that you may want to explore.

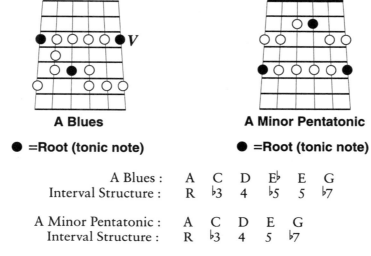

A Blues   **A Minor Pentatonic**

● =Root (tonic note)   ● =Root (tonic note)

A Blues :	A	C	D	E♭	E	G
Interval Structure :	R	♭3	4	♭5	5	♭7

A Minor Pentatonic :	A	C	D	E	G
Interval Structure :	R	♭3	4	5	♭7

Scale Choices for Section B.

The A blues scale can used throughout this section. For A5, A7, and D/A try the A major pentatonic scale. For G5, and G6 (No 3rd) try the G major pentatonic scale.

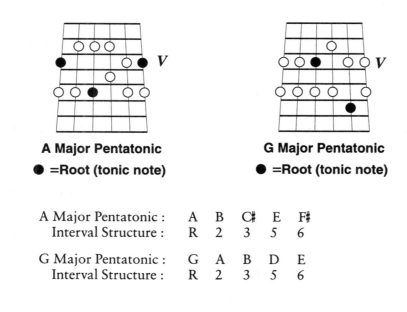

A Major Pentatonic   **G Major Pentatonic**

● =Root (tonic note)   ● =Root (tonic note)

A Major Pentatonic :	A	B	C#	E	F#
Interval Structure :	R	2	3	5	6

G Major Pentatonic :	G	A	B	D	E
Interval Structure :	R	2	3	5	6

Scale Choices for Section C.

For Em7

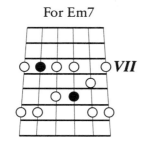

E Minor Pentatonic
● =Root (tonic note)

For F#m7

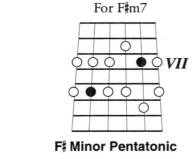

F# Minor Pentatonic
● =Root (tonic note)

For G5

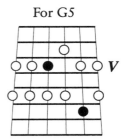

G Major Pentatonic
● =Root (tonic note)

For A5, A/C#

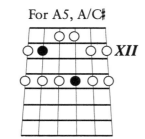

A Major Pentatonic
● =Root (tonic note)

For Bm7, D, D/C

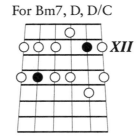

B Minor Pentatonic
● =Root (tonic note)

For D/C

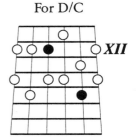

D Mixolydian Pentatonic
● =Root (tonic note)

D Mixolydian pentatonic is a modal idea. Take a major pentatonic scale and raise the 6th note to a ♭7 (B to C).

Arpeggio Choices for Section C.

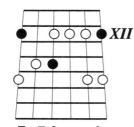

Em7 Arpeggio
E G B D
● =Root (tonic note)

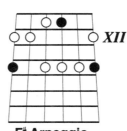

F# Arpeggio
F# A C# E
● =Root (tonic note)

G Arpeggio
G B D
● =Root (tonic note)

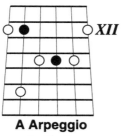

A Arpeggio
A C# E
● =Root (tonic note)

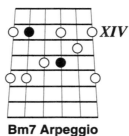

Bm7 Arpeggio
B D F# A
● =Root (tonic note)

D7 Arpeggio
D F# A C
● =Root (tonic note)

The Grooveyard

On this composition, the main section I want to cover is the Solo Section. (The majority of the song is built around a melody riff, and the main theme of the song is built around G blues.)

Scale Choices for Solo Section.

You could try the D blues scale for D5.

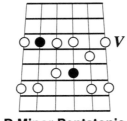

D Minor Pentatonic

● =Root (tonic note)

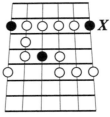

D Blues

● =Root (tonic note)

D Minor Pentatonic :	D	F	G	A	C	
Interval Structure :	R	♭3	4	5	♭7	
D Blues :	D	F	G	A♭	A	C
Interval Structure :	R	♭3	4	♭5	5	♭7

For B5, I went a different route and saw it as a dominant 7, even though the B5 chord doesn't necessarily imply that. Remember: Root-and-5th power chords don't tell you whether the chord is major or minor, because the 3rd is not in the chord.

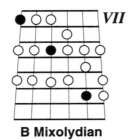

B Mixolydian

● =Root (tonic note)

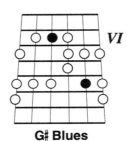

G♯ Blues

● =Root (tonic note)

B Mixolydian :	B	C♯	D♯	E	F♯	G♯	A
Interval Structure :	R	2	3	4	5	6	♭7
G♯ Blues (B Major Blues Sound) :	G♯	B	C♯	D	D♯	F♯	
Interval Structure :	6	R	2	♭3/♯9	3	5	

Arpeggio Choices

Based the scale information the following arpeggio choices could be used. Since the D5 chord implies a minor sound, the five tonic- note patterns for Dm are:

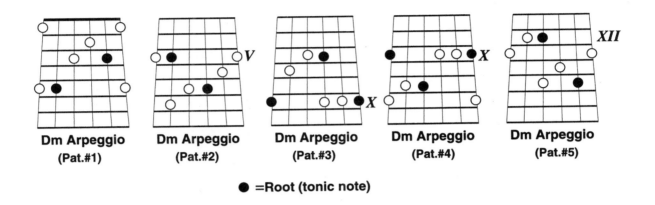

Dm Arpeggio
(Pat.#1)

Dm Arpeggio
(Pat.#2)

Dm Arpeggio
(Pat.#3)

Dm Arpeggio
(Pat.#4)

Dm Arpeggio
(Pat.#5)

● =Root (tonic note)

Dm Arpeggio:	D	F	A
Interval Structure:	R	♭3	5

Since the B5 chord is being treated like a dominant 7th chord , try using a dominant 7 arpeggio.

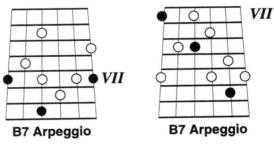

B7 Arpeggio

B7 Arpeggio

● =Root (tonic note)

B7 Arpeggio:	B	D♯	F♯	A
Interval Structure:	R	3	5	♭7

About The Author

The career of Marc Cooper (A.K.A. Coop De Ville) has seen him perform in concert, clubs and studios throughout the U.S., Canada, Europe, Japan, China, Vietnam, Thailand, and Indonesia.He has won numerous guitar competitions such as the 1994 Washburn guitars/JamTrax Hot Guitarist Competition at the NAMM show in Los Angeles and the Fender Guitar Warz'89 and '90 and the Yamaha Guitar Warz'91.He has performed on stage with Joe Walsh, Danny Gatton, Seymour Duncan, Gregg Bissonette (drummer for Joe Satriani, and David Lee Roth), Steve Howe (of Yes, and Asia), Carmine Appice (drummer for Rod Stewart, and Jeff Beck) and Rob Affuso (drummer for Skid Row), Pat Travers, blues sensation Rita Chiarelli, bassist Alphonso Johnson, Michel Cusson, and many others.

In 1982, Coop graduated from G.I.T. (Guitar Institute of Technology) where he had studied with Howard Roberts, Ron Eschete, Don Mock, Robben Ford, Steve Morse, Pat Martino, Tommy Tedesco, Mick Gooderick, and Joe Pass, among many other teachers.

In 1995, Coop released his debut CD, Coop De Ville: Shelter from the Storm. He followed it up with a second release entitled, Speaking in other Tongues. He is an active international clinician for Digitech and Godin guitars.Coop endorses Godin guitars, Digitech effects and preamps, DOD pedals, Musitech electronics, 2 Tek bridges, Sabine tuners, Charlie Stringer Strings, and Emu synth modules.